Faith-Filled Fun & Games for Drivetime

Joy Ride!

Faith-Filled Fun & Games for Drivetime

by
Jacqueline Lederman

Tyndale House Publishers, Wheaton, Illinois

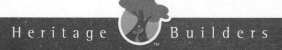

Heritage Builders

JOY RIDE!

Library of Congress Cataloging-in-Publication Data

Lederman, Jacqueline.
Joy ride! : faith-filled fun & games for drivetime / by Jacqueline
Lederman.
p. cm. — (Heritage builders)
"A Focus on the Family book"—T.p. verso.
Includes bibliographical references and indexes.
ISBN 1–56179–798–7
1. Games in Christian education. 2. Bible games and puzzles. 3.
Games for travelers. 4. Family recreation. I. Title. II. Series.

BV1536.3 .L43 2000
249—dc21

00–020638

A Focus on the Family book published by Tyndale House Publishers,
Wheaton, Illinois.

For Lightwave
Concept Design and Direction: Rick Osborne
Managing Editor: Elaine Osborne
Text Director: K. Christie Bowler
Art Director: Terry Van Roon
Desktop Publisher: Andrew Jaster
Editorial Assistants: Mikal Clarke, Ed Strauss

Cover Design: Steve Diggs & Friends, Nashville

Printed in the United States of America

00 01 02 03 04 05/10 9 8 7 6 5 4 3 2 1

Table of Contents

Bible Challenges

Indexes

Introduction

The fact that you have this book in your hand says three things:

1. You have children.

2. You want them to be learning more about the Bible.

3. You want to trade in your imaginary duct tape for good family times. (You know—the duct tape you wish you could use on your kids to keep them quiet sometimes.)

Within these pages you will find a variety of new and interesting ways to help you teach your children while you enjoy quality time together on the road. The goal of this book is to provide families with a good Christian growth resource to use in the car. *Joy Ride!* is comprised of three sections: games, discussion starters, and Bible challenges.

GAMES

The first section contains a variety of games you can play in the car, from typical license plate games to more active and involved ones. Playing these travel games can be a fun way to learn new information and use creative thinking to stretch children spiritually.

Scoring is suggested as a means to motivate players to participate and do their best. A simple baseline scoring is suggested. Depending on the makeup of your family, you can adjust this scoring to heighten the competition or discourage it.

What kind of rewards, if any, should you use? It largely depends on what motivates your children. For very short trips, where you play only one game, it's probably enough just to be declared the winner. But if you need more incentive, candy is a popular motivator! For trips where you play a few games, it might be good to have small rewards, such as a peanut M&M for each point scored. Or you could purchase a bag of wrapped juice gummies to stick in the glove compartment, where it's handy when you need a reward.

On long trips it's nice to have a special treat for a reward. For instance, perhaps you promise an ice-cream cone to everyone who earns at least 20 points at the end of an afternoon. The winner could choose the place to stop (such as McDonald's or Dairy Queen). However you choose to arrange it, have fun!

DISCUSSION STARTERS

Discussion starters are designed to start intriguing, exciting, and enjoyable discussions as you travel. It's a good idea to read them before you begin your drive as it may be difficult to refer to the discussion starters if you are the driver. If you have older children who can read well, hand them the book. If your children are too young to read this book, then it may be best to have a simplified discussion. So take a minute or two to prepare your discussion before you start driving by quickly reading through the starter you are going to use.

Start the discussion off by relating the "Jump Start" to your passengers. Once the children have started talking, you begin "Speeding Up" with additional points and questions. "Look at the Map" takes you to see what God's Word says about that topic. Then you can conclude your discussion with a "Travel Plan" to bring the discussion around to what your children can do about it in their lives. Drivetimes are great moments to impress spiritual things on your children, if you take advantage of them.

At the bottom of the discussion starters, where relevant, you will find references to other starters, games, or challanges that deal with a similar subject.

BIBLE CHALLENGES

Bible challenges contain lots of interesting Bible quizzes and trivia. Instructions accompany each section. Use the challenges merely to have fun or to start conversations about a variety of subjects. The information in the questions and answers will add to your children's knowledge of the Bible in an enjoyable and challenging way.

The New International Version of the Bible is used throughout *Joy Ride!* If you use an alternate version, there may be times when a slightly different answer will appear in your Bible. Sometimes a second version can be helpful to increase understanding of the text, and you can talk about that.

How to Use This Book

It might be a good idea to let your children know what this book is and how you're using it: that these are biblically based games, discussion starters ("car-versations"), and trivia. Emphasize that these games will be lots of fun as well as help them learn more about God's Word. With some children, if you don't let them know this, they will expect something else and might feel disappointed, frustrated, or tricked when you begin introducing "Bible stuff" into what they thought would be pure fun. With other children, however, you might want to use the book in a very laid-back fashion, without verbalizing what you are trying to accomplish with them. They will still learn but with less awareness of the process. However, make sure your children never feel deceived or manipulated into learning biblical things. The choice of approach is yours: you know your children best, and you know which route would be most effective with them.

Enjoyable learning will stick with your children and they'll ask for more. Sometimes you can play the games just for fun, without making them biblically oriented, but when your turn comes, you can choose a biblical word or item to encourage your children to think along those lines.

If your children are at different ages or skill levels, don't always play the games with the whole family. Doing so would discourage the younger or less skilled ones since the older ones would get all the answers. Give the younger ones their own questions at their skill level. If you are trying to include everyone in the discussion, ask specific children to answer certain questions. Get your older children involved as facilitators or coaches to the younger ones, or make them play with a handicap (for example, they have to spell their answers, act them out, talk backwards).

Some of the games, starters, or challenge sections tie in nicely with others in the book. Use the indexes in the back of the book to find particular topics. Choose topics that are relevant to your children and are of current interest, and pursue them through the various games and activities.

Truths need to be applied, so be aware of possibilities for making practical applications as they arise naturally out of your discussions and games. Keep the question "How is this 'car-versation' going to affect who we are and how we do things?" in mind. Or make up an application. For example, "Now that we understand this, when someone does something that makes you feel upset, don't explode. Ask God to help you calm down and know how to respond to that person." Possible applications will often be suggested with the activities.

A word of caution. You are wise not to make every trip in the car into a Bible learning time, and not to make every game or discussion end with a pointed moral lesson. Use your drivetimes to develop your relationships with your children and find out how they are doing, how their friends are, what they're up to, and so on.

LISTENING: A SKILL TO BE LEARNED, ON THE ROAD OR OFF

Positive interactions with your children begin with how well you hear what they have to say. Here are some pointers on being an active listener in or out of your vehicle, thereby teaching your children how to listen as well:

- Let others finish talking before you start.
- Learn to ask open-ended questions that encourage discussion rather than closed ones that call for one-word answers.
- Realize that just as you think what you have to say is the most important (and it probably is), the other person thinks what he or she has to say is the most important too (and it probably is also).
- No one will find you interesting until he or she finds you interested.
- Your way is not the only way.

Show your children that you are interested in them and that you care for them. Your attention, body language, eye contact (although not when driving), and facial expressions all reveal if you are really interested in what they are saying. Teach your children how to listen by your example.

Games

License Plate Game

This is a good game to play when the traffic is moving slowly, so you can look at the license plates longer.

Players look at the license plates they see, then make up words with the letters and call them out. Most license plates contain letters as well as numbers. Players can't change the order of the letters on the license plate, but they can add any letters needed to make a word. If they make a word that has to do with the Bible, a Bible character or place, or the Christian life, they get extra points (not just words like "first, go, work" that might appear in the Bible but are general).

For example, the plate MRC 554 could yield the word "miracle" or "mercy."

Score one point to everyone who makes up words, and one extra point for each biblical word.

An alternative is to form phrases instead of words. In this case, each letter of the license plate should be the first letter of a word in the phrase.

For example, the plate JML 633 could yield the phrase "Jesus, my Lord."

I Look, I See

This can be played easily on both short or long trips.

This is a game where family members notice their environment as they drive and try to see something that rhymes with a biblical object.

For example, they might see a park and call out, "Park, ark," or see a cable and call out, "Cable, stable."

Score one point to each participant and one extra point to the person calling out the most answers.

Word Games

You can play this anytime, but when Bibles are handy, such as on the way to church, children might come up with ideas more quickly.

One person thinks of a biblical compound word or a two- to three-word phrase. He or she tells the others only half of the word or only one word of the phrase. The others have to guess the whole thing. If they haven't gotten it after a number of guesses, they can ask a few questions.

Example 1: If the person said, "Make," they might ask, "Is it _____ make or make _____?" "Is it one word or a phrase?" The answer could have been "make friends" or "make disciples."

Example 2: If the person said, "Sabbath," they might ask, "Is it _____ Sabbath or Sabbath _____?" "Is it a command?" "Is it an occasion?" The answer could have been "Lord of the Sabbath," "Sabbath Day," "Honor the Sabbath," "Sabbath-rest," or "Keep the Sabbath."

Score one point to each participant and one additional point to the person who correctly guesses the most.

Name That Tune

Play this anytime.

Below is a list of hymns and other Christian songs you can use for this game. You can play this game three ways.

A. Read the title of a song, and the first person who can hum the beginning of the song correctly wins the point. *Score one point to each winner.*

B. Have a person begin by humming the first few lines to the song. The one who guesses what song it is first wins. *Score one point to each winner.*

C. One person says the first line of the song, and whoever can say or sing the second line wins. *Score one point to each winner.*

Please don't be discouraged if you aren't a particularly musical family. Just have fun trying. The Bible tells us in Psalm 33:1: "Sing joyfully to the LORD, you righteous; it is fitting for the upright to praise him."

SAMPLE SONGS

1. AMAZING GRACE
Amazing grace, how sweet the sound
That saved a wretch like me.

2. GO TELL IT ON THE MOUNTAIN
Go tell it on the mountain,
Over the hills and everywhere.

3. GOD IS SO GOOD
God is so good,
God is so good.

4. JOY TO THE WORLD
Joy to the world,
The Lord is come.

5. KUM BA YA
Kum ba ya, my Lord,
Kum ba ya.

6. MICHAEL ROW THE BOAT ASHORE
Michael row the boat ashore.
Hallelujah.

7. THE LORD'S PRAYER
Our Father
Which art in heaven.

8. O HOLY NIGHT
O holy night,
The stars are brightly shining.

9. O LITTLE TOWN OF BETHLEHEM
O little town of Bethlehem,
How still we see thee lie.

10. PRAISE GOD FROM WHOM ALL BLESSINGS FLOW
Praise God from whom all blessings flow,
Praise Him all creatures here below.

11. ROCK OF AGES
Rock of ages
Cleft for me.

12. WE GATHER TOGETHER
We gather together
To ask the Lord's blessing.

13. WHAT A FRIEND WE HAVE IN JESUS
What a friend we have in Jesus,
All our sins and griefs to bear.

Journal Keeping

This is especially good on long trips for children who like to doodle and for those who are motivated by longer-term rewards.

Make a game out of keeping a journal of your trip. Provide a small notebook or scratch pad to each of your children, and encourage them to draw pictures of things God has made that they see on your journey—or they can write about their experiences. After each stop they can begin a new page, describing where they stopped or drawing a picture.

You could also encourage your children to pick a leaf at each stop and do a leaf rubbing on the journal pages. They can do this by placing the leaf under the page in the journal and rubbing the side of the pencil gently over the page where the leaf lies underneath. Alternative objects to rub include shells, coins, walls, tombstones, and rocks.

Score one point for each page done.

All-Day I-Spy

This is for longer trips.

Pick one item from either list below to concentrate on for the day. The first person to see that situation or object each time calls it out throughout the day. You can decide if you would like to include pictures on billboards or not. (For some of the symbols, you definitely would need to include pictures.)

SITUATION LIST (PICK ONE)

- A person being helpful
- A child being obedient
- Two or more people laughing together
- Someone at a church
- Someone singing

OBJECT LIST (PICK ONE)

- Church—where Christians everywhere go to worship and meet together with other believers.
- Cross—a powerful symbol of the supreme sacrifice Jesus made for the sins of the world.
- Fish—symbol (ICHTHUS) used by believers in the early days of persecution as a secret sign. One person

would draw an arc in the sand, and the other would complete the sign to show their shared faith. ICHTHUS is Greek from letters in the phrase "Jesus Christ, Son of God, Savior," and it means "fish."

- Crown—symbol of royal authority. Christ is our King of kings.
- Rainbow—symbol of God's faithfulness.
- Rock—symbol of Christ, our solid rock.
- Tower—symbol of God, our refuge.

Keep a running total and score one point each time to the person who spies the selected situation or object.

Biblical Letter Ladder

This can be played on a short trip to the store.

A player thinks of any biblical word, then says its first letter only, such as *t* for "trouble." The second player thinks of a biblical word beginning with *t* and adds a second letter from the word he or she was thinking of, such as *e* for "tempt." The next player adds a third letter to try to form the continuation of a real biblical word. When a player completes a word, the round ends. Sometimes a person will be unable to add another letter; that person is then out of the round. Play continues until someone completes a word or all players are out. Start a new round with a new letter.

All players receive one point. The one who completes the word gets one additional point.

Guess the Character

This is good for any length trip.

One person chooses a Bible character whom he or she knows quite a bit about. That person will need to give clues about this character to help the others guess who it is. Have the person start by giving only one clue. He or she can give additional clues as they are needed until someone guesses the correct answer.

For example, give clues such as "friend of Jesus, writer, had a brother." The answer is John.

Scoring: All participants score one point, and one extra point goes to the one correctly guessing the most.

Bible Anagrams

Best for older children.

An anagram is a word or phrase formed by rearranging the letters of another word or phrase. The making of anagrams as a game has been played since ancient times. Try to make up your own biblical anagrams. This can be hard, and older children might enjoy the challenge of searching their Bibles for ideas and taking time to rearrange letters into a new word to stump their opponents.

For example, someone finds the word "parted" in the Bible (such as from the story where God parted the sea) and turns it into "depart." The other players are told the anagram, "depart," and attempt to rearrange the letters to form the original word the first person found in the Bible.

Score one point to everyone who makes up an anagram, and one point to each one who solves an anagram.

Synonyms

This is an easy game to play on short trips. More suitable for older children, although the younger ones can participate and learn.

To play, participants must think of a synonym (another word that has a similar meaning) for each word in the list below. Players call out the synonyms they think of. When you have exhausted this list, you can add additional words of your own.

Love	Joy	Peace
Patience	Kindness	Goodness
Faithfulness	Gentleness	Self-control
Spiritual	Freedom	Righteousness
Judgment	Knowledge	Wisdom
Repentance	Truth	Rejoice
Wrath	Glory	Splendor
Commandment	Consequences	Devoted
Serving	Contributing	Generously
Endurance	Encouragement	Acceptable
Foundation	Refreshed	Perishable
Comforting	Blameless	Purpose
Deliverance	Instruction	Appoint
Radiance	Sacrifice	Covenant

For example, if you pick the word "love," players will call out a word that they think means something similar, such as "charity" or "care." Then you go on to the next word.

Score one point to all participants, and score one extra point to the person who thinks of synonyms for the most words.

Opposites

This game is easy to play on short trips. It's more suitable for older children, although the younger ones can participate and learn.

Use the following list to play a game of opposites, where players must think of a word that means the opposite of the given word. You may think of additional words as well.

Love	Joy	Peace
Patience	Kindness	Trustworthy
Honest	Humble	Hospitable
Generous	Commendable	Meek
Temperamental	Thankful	Holy
Blameless	Wicked	Confidence
Rejoicing	Sick	Godly
Sincere	Despair	Servant

For example, if you pick the word "joy," players will call out a word that they think means the opposite, such as "sad" or "unhappy." Then you go on to the next word.

Score one point to all participants. If played competitively, score one extra point to the person who thinks of opposites for the most words.

Second Timothy
License Plate Bingo

This is a letter game that even nonreaders can play if someone tells them what they're looking for. Good for longer trips. You can use other verses that you would like to teach your children as well—a fun way to help them memorize.

Have all players write down the following verse on a piece of paper: "'I have fought the good fight, I have finished the race, I have kept the faith' (2 Timothy 4:7)." Using only the letters seen on license plates, players cross off the letters and numbers on their sheet as they see them. First to cross off all the letters and numbers wins. For example, if a player sees the license plate TGF 332, he or she can cross off the "T" in "Timothy," the "g" in "good," the "f" in "fight," and the "2" in "2 Timothy."

Score one point to all participants, and the winner receives one additional point. Also give one extra point to anyone who can recite the verse from memory at the end of play.

Ezra

This is tricky at first. Have some laughs and keep trying. Children need to know their multiplication tables to be able to play this game.

Ezra is a book of the Bible that is full of details. This is a game of watching the details. Ezra is most entertaining when played as fast as possible. The principle of play is that the name Ezra is substituted in place of an agreed-upon biblical number, such as three, seven, or twelve. Talk about what is biblical about that number; then players begin taking turns counting and replacing the chosen number with the name Ezra. When someone messes up, the round is over. A new biblical number can be chosen before starting again.

For example, let's say the number three is suggested. First talk about things in the Bible that have to do with three (for example, the three men in the fiery furnace in Daniel 3, the three persons of the Trinity). Then the first player counts off "one"; the second player, "two"; and the third player says "Ezra" instead of "three."

Any time a number that is a multiple of three comes up, the player must say "Ezra" or drop out of play. Also, if a number contains a three but is not a multiple of three, only the "three" is replaced by "Ezra." So the number 13 would be "Ezra-teen," the number 53 would be "fifty-Ezra," and the number 33 would be "Ezra, Ezra."

Score one point to each participant and one extra point to each round winner.

Bible Comic Strip Fun

Good to play on longer trips for those young artists among you.

Some children can spend lots of time drawing while riding on trips. A fun drawing activity is to have them make their own comic strips. Have them choose a Bible story to illustrate in little blocks on paper and write captions, just like a regular comic strip.

Some suggestions of good stories to illustrate are:
- Jonah (book of Jonah).
- David and Goliath (1 Samuel 17).
- Jesus' death and resurrection (Matthew 27–28).
- The Good Samaritan (Luke 10:30–35).

Score one point to everyone who spends time drawing a comic strip.

Twelve Spy
Good for short or long car trips.

Twelve is a significant number in the Bible.

There were 12 tribes of Israel and 12 disciples of Jesus, to name two examples. Can you think of others? Pick an item that you will use as the object to count for the game, and see who can find 12 of that object first.

For example, maybe you pick red pickup trucks as your object for one round of the game. Then on the word "Go!" everyone will quietly be counting red pickup trucks until they get to 12. The winner says, "Twelve spy"—not 12 spies!

To continue playing, pick a new object and start again. Other ideas to get you going are buses, food trucks, station wagons, hotel signs, and cars that have something hanging from the rearview mirror.

Score one point to each participant. Give one additional point to the winner of each round.

Name Search
This is something for the child who likes to play the "investigator" and likes to read in the car. It is good for short trips with Bibles in hand.

This game is the most fun when it is done quickly. Have the children locate a person's name in the Bible that starts with *A*, such as Adam or Abraham. The first one to find such a name then announces the name and where it was found. Then players go on to search for a name that begins with the *last* letter of the name that was just announced. Start with five minutes, and if the interest is still there, continue another five minutes. Challenge the children to find more than 20 names within five minutes!

For example, if someone finds Adam, they would say something like "Adam—Genesis 2:20. M is the last letter." Then the children search for a name beginning with *M*, and so on, until the time limit is up.

Score one point to all participants and one extra point to the person who finds the most names, if you want to keep track.

Categories

This is a fun game to play for any length trip. Select the simpler categories for younger children.

Pick a category from the list below of things mentioned in the Bible. Then take turns naming one item in that category found in the Bible. You can set a time limit, such as 30 seconds, to respond on a turn. Eliminate players from the round when they cannot come up with an answer.

For example, let's say that "foods" is the chosen category. The first person might say, "Bread." The next person might say, "Manna." And so on.

Score one point to all participants.

LIST OF BIBLE CATEGORIES

Animals	Books of the Bible	Children
Cities/Countries	Commands	Disciples
Foods	Good actions	Judges
Kings	Miracles of Jesus	Men
Plants and trees	Prophets	Sins
Stones	Stories	Women

Alphabet Bible Names

Especially good for highway trips. Play it twice in a row and see how many new names you can think of.

To play, begin with the letter *A*. The first person to think of a biblical name that begins with *A* calls it out. Then go on to the letter *B*. The first person to think of a biblical name beginning with *B* calls it out, and so on. You may find you need to skip a letter if no one can think of an answer after two minutes of trying. However, it is possible to think of a name for every letter, if you use names of God as well! If you get stuck, you can refer to page 30 for examples for names beginning with each letter.

For example, someone might call out "Adam," then someone calls out "Barabbas," and so on.

Score one point to each participant and one extra point to a winner if you wish to keep track and determine who answered the most.

Twenty Questions

This is great to play on long trips, but it can be played anytime with all ages.

One person thinks of a person, place, or thing from the Bible that he or she knows quite a bit about, but keeps it a secret. The others ask questions that need a yes or no answer to figure out what it is the person is thinking of. The only thing the first person can say is "Yes" or "No." The others have up to 20 questions to try to figure out the answer. Take turns being "it."

For example, Mom might start by thinking of a dove. The other players begin asking questions like: "Is it a living thing?" "Is it bigger than the car?" "Do we have one?"

Score one point to each participant and one additional point to the player who wins each round.

What Book Am I?

Use this for any length trip.

People think of a book in the Bible that they are capable of giving clues about. Have them give one clue at a time until someone finally guesses the correct book.

For example, "I'm thinking of a book in the Bible that is a letter. It's not written by Paul. It is in the New Testament. It starts with the letter J. It is found after the book of Hebrews." (The answer would be James.)

Score one point to each participant and one extra point to the one correctly guessing the most.

Forty on the Map

This is good for longer trips when you've got destinations on the brain and maps handy.

Give each child a map—or give them all one large map to share, if this won't cause a problem. Set the kids on a hunt to find as many 40s on the map as possible and circle them with a pencil. You can also do this with other significant biblical numbers.

The 40s might be a number of a road, a mile count between two points, an exit number, whatever. They should just find as many 40s as they can in a given amount of time—perhaps 10 minutes. When the children have finished their hunt, read the following examples of the significance of the number 40 in the Bible. Perhaps you can think of others.

Examples:
1. The Lord made it rain for 40 days and 40 nights when He sent the Flood.
2. The Israelites spent 40 years wandering in the wilderness because of their stubborn ways and disobedience.
3. Jesus was in the desert for 40 days just after He was baptized by John the Baptist. He was tempted by Satan. But guess what—He didn't give in or sin in any way!
4. Jesus went back into heaven 40 days after His resurrection from the dead.

Score a point for each participant and one extra point to the person who finds the most 40s.

Alphabet Thankfulness

Anytime is a great time to play this game for all ages.

This is also good to play on longer trips with paper and pencil for older children. They can write out their lists and then compare notes.

Starting with *A*, each person names something starting with that letter that they can be thankful God made or has provided for them. Then *B*, and so on. You are sure to get some silly answers because your kids may be thankful for some unexpected items!

Examples: A—Aunt Pat, B—Brothers, C—Chocolate.
Score one point to all participants. If played competitively,

score one additional point to the person who thinks of something for the most letters.

Blow the Chaff

Play with children who are easily amused and need a little excitement.

This is a silly game worth a few minutes of fun. Explain that the Bible describes the wicked as chaff that the wind blows away. Chaff is a part of the wheat kernel that is not eaten. It is so light that it blows away easily when the wheat is crushed.

Each player should tear a small piece of paper (about two inches across) and hold the piece above his or her head. Then, on the count of three, have a contest to see who can blow, blow, blow upward on their "chaff" to keep it airborne the longest.

Score one point to all participants and one extra point to the winner.

I Spy Colors

Good imagination game for younger children as well as older.

Take turns spying the color of a vehicle, sign, house, whatever, and say what that color might represent from the Bible.

For example, a child sees a red Corvette drive past and says, "I spy red, the color of Jesus' blood." "I spy yellow, the color of the sun God made."

Score one point to each participant and one extra point to the person who spies the most biblical colors.

Here's a Pair, There's a Pair

Play this anytime, on short trips or long.

There are all sorts of twosomes in the Bible. Take turns thinking of one part of a biblical pair and let the other players guess the second half.

For example, someone says, "Adam." The correct response would, of course, be "Eve." Other examples include "tithes and offerings" and "Sodom and Gomorrah."

Score one point to all participants and one extra point to the person who guesses or thinks of the most biblical pairs.

Books of the Bible Scramble

*Good for longer trips. Play this with children who can
spell and write and don't get carsick.*

Use the scrambled names of books of the Bible below. Give
paper pads to the children and see how long it takes for them to
unscramble the names correctly after one person reads the
scrambled letters aloud. Alternatively, read out a list of the
scrambled book letters so that the children can write them
down and then work on them. Allow children to use their Bibles
if needed. It may be too overwhelming to do all the books at
one time, unless you have real go-getters. You may want to
assign them just a portion of the numbers, such as 1–10 or
30–40 to work on at a given time—or just tell them to see how
many they can complete. When they get tired, they'll stop.
Answers are found at the end of the Games section on page 30.

1. KELU
2. CLESNRHCOI 1 & 2
3. UTSIT
4. ITONEALRVE
5. SMSLPA
6. EASMJ
7. ILMAAHC
8. TNIASOMLNAET
9. PNHAEIHAZ
10. BSOVRERP
11. NSASISOCLO
12. RSMBNUE
13. ANMUH
14. SEJUGD
15. SOSSNNALHTEAI 1 & 2
16. OJEL
17. THISCRANOIN 1 & 2
18. SMULEA 1 & 2
19. MIREAHJE

20. DEUSXO
21. BJO
22. GAGIAH
23. AHSIAI
24. INADLE
25. ICMHA
26. UHJOSA
27. WTHTMAE
28. TREEP 1 & 2
29. GSON FO SSGON
30. TCAS
31. EOHAS
32. HIMPLNOE
33. RSHETE
34. KARM
35. STIUCILEV
36. KABKAHUK
37. OHNJ
38. CHEZRIHAA

39. NOAHJ
40. SAMO
41. SBWERHE
42. GINKS 1 & 2
43. UHRT
44. TYIHOMT 1 & 2
45. ENIGESS
46. EJDU
47. TAGLNSAAI
48. EIMHEHAN
49. SSPEANIHE
50. OHNJ 1, 2, 3
51. SCSLTEACEIES
52. PLSIPAHPIIN
53. RYOMOTNEUDE
54. AHBIOAD
55. SNARMO
56. RAEZ
57. ZEELIEK

*Score one point to each participant and one additional point to
the child who either finishes first or unscrambles the most books.*

What Book Comes Next?

Play anytime you have a Bible handy for reference.

Take turns calling out any book of the Bible and see who can be first to respond correctly with the book that comes after it in the Bible.

For example, someone calls out, "Matthew." The correct response would be "Mark."

Score one point to all participants and one point to the person who correctly answers the most.

Good Scents

This game is good for medium or longer trips.

Below are listed some Bible references of verses that talk about things with particular smells. You can look up a few to set the stage for this game or simply read some things from the list to get your children's interest. It is clear that God gave us the ability to smell because it is something that He enjoys as well.

- Genesis 8:20–21—Burnt offerings
- Exodus 30:37–38—Incense
- Leviticus 3:16—An offering made by fire
- Song of Songs 2:13—Blossoming vines
- Matthew 2:11—Incense and myrrh
- John 12:3—Perfume
- 2 Corinthians 2:15—Us!

See who can find the most items that have a scent or smell by looking out of the window. You can find items that are pictured on signs or other items along the road. Just call out what is seen and tell whether it is a good or a bad scent. Try not to repeat answers that someone else has given. Use this lighthearted game to talk about discerning good from bad, just as you go about determining whether something produces a good or a bad smell.

For example, someone might see a sign with a picture of a cheeseburger and say, "Cheeseburger—good smell!" and so on.

Score one point for participating.

True or False

Young children love this game.

Make some statements to your children. Some will be true and some will be false, some biblical and some not. You can make some statements that are silly and some that are serious. Your children are to reply "True!" or "False!"

Examples:
- Bees hibernate in the winter. (False)
- Ten times three equals 30. (True)
- Christ hung on the cross for three days. (False)
- According to the Bible, Job lived an easy life. (False)
- Cain was Adam and Eve's first son. (True)

Score one point to each participant and one extra point to the child with the most correct responses.

Decoding Fun

Most appropriate for longer trips and older children who don't get sick from reading in moving vehicles.

On pieces of paper, children decode the following Scripture verses. These verses can be written out on the paper ahead of time (before you start your trip in the car), or an adult can read the letters out carefully as the children write them down. (Numbers are not coded.) Replace each letter with the letter that precedes it in the alphabet.

For example, QFBDFNBLFST would translate to PEACE-MAKERS. (P precedes Q, E precedes F, etc.)

After the children have decoded the verses below, they can be challenged to "code" new verses themselves and then exchange with someone for more decoding fun.

"QFBDFNBLFST XIP TPX JO QFBDF SBJTF B IBSWFTU PG SJHIUFPVTOFTT" (KBNFT 3:18).

"J BN UIF BMQIB BOE UIF PNFHB…" (SFWFMBUJPO 1:8).

"UIFSF JT OP XJTEPN, OP JOTJHIU, OP QMBO UIBU DBO TVDDFFE BHBJOTU UIF MPSE" (QSPWFSCT 21:30).

"XIBUFWFS ZPV EJE GPS POF PG UIF MFBTU PG UIFTF CSPUIFST PG NJOE, ZPV EJE GPS NF" (NBUUIFX 25:40).

Score one point to each participant and one extra point to the person who decodes the most verses.

Catch a Smile

Play anytime the kids are in a "smile-y" mood—or perhaps when they're not, to create a smile in them!

Proverbs 15:13 says, "A happy heart makes the face cheerful, but heartache crushes the spirit."

The challenge of this game is to see how many people your children can catch smiling. They can encourage some people to be cheerful by giving them a smile. The children may look for people either in other cars or along the streets. You don't want your children to make anyone uncomfortable by staring at them, but they might be able to brighten some-one's face just by giving them a nice smile. Spread some cheer and catch some smiles.

Score one point for every participant and one extra point to the winner of the most smiles.

The Be-Attitude

Good for traveling where there are lots of signs.

Everyone is to look at signs for words that can be used to complete the statement "Be _____" in ways that are positive and match what God wants them to be.

For example, you might see a sign that says "the great adventure"; you can use the word "great" to call out, "Be great!"

Score one point to each participant and one extra point to the person who makes the most "be-attitudes."

Scavenger Hunt

You can make up other lists of your own after you've played this one. This game is best played on longer trips.

Go down the following list, one item at a time, and see who can find all five items first.

1. A person driving within the speed limit
2. A Christian bumper sticker or symbol
3. A person acting kindly
4. A sign with the word "love"
5. A license plate with the number 12

Score one point to all participants and one extra point to the winner.

Sounds Like a Proverb

Good game for driving through a city or on a stretch of highway with lots of signs.

Have children make up proverbs, or wise sayings, from something that they see on a sign or bumper sticker.

For example, you might see an advertisement for an airline. You could say, "Make sure that what you place your trust in will not let you fall." Perhaps you see a picture of someone taking a bite of fruit. You could say, "Fruit is good for the body, as obedience is good for the soul."

Score one point to each participant and one extra point to the person who makes up the most proverbs.

Story Lines

Best if you have a Bible handy.

Go around the circle of people in your vehicle, telling a Bible story. Each person can add only one sentence to the story at a time. Encourage by example to go into detail of what the character might have been feeling or experiencing in that situation.

For example, Daniel in the Lion's Den: "Once there was a young man named Daniel .... Daniel was very brave .... Daniel loved God a lot .... It made some of the men angry who worked for the king .... Some men tried to trick the king ...."

Choose stories that deal with particular subjects you might want to discuss.

Score a point to each person who participates with a good attitude for each story.

SAMPLE ANSWERS FOR ALPHABET BIBLE NAMES, PAGE 21.

Adam	Barnabas	Caleb
Deborah	Elijah	Felix
Gideon	Herod	Isaac
Jacob	King of Kings	Lazarus
Mary	Naomi	Obadiah
Paul	Queen Esther	Rachel
Stephen	Timothy	Uriah
Vashti	Wonderful	Xerxes
Yahweh	Zacchaeus	

ANSWERS FOR BOOKS OF THE BIBLE SCRAMBLE, PAGE 25.

1. Luke
2. 1 & 2 Chronicles
3. Titus
4. Revelation
5. Psalms
6. James
7. Malachi
8. Lamentations
9. Zephaniah
10. Proverbs
11. Colossians
12. Numbers
13. Nahum
14. Judges
15. 1 & 2 Thessalonians
16. Joel
17. 1 & 2 Corinthians
18. 1 & 2 Samuel
19. Jeremiah
20. Exodus
21. Job
22. Haggai
23. Isaiah
24. Daniel
25. Micah
26. Joshua
27. Matthew
28. 1 & 2 Peter
29. Song of Songs
30. Acts
31. Hosea
32. Philemon
33. Esther
34. Mark
35. Leviticus
36. Habakkuk
37. John
38. Zechariah
39. Jonah
40. Amos
41. Hebrews
42. 1 & 2 Kings
43. Ruth
44. 1 & 2 Timothy
45. Genesis
46. Jude
47. Galatians
48. Nehemiah
49. Ephesians
50. 1, 2, 3 John
51. Ecclesiastes
52. Philippians
53. Deuteronomy
54. Obadiah
55. Romans
56. Ezra
57. Ezekiel

Discussion Starters

Boiling Mad

JUMP START:

Let's say you're driving along and the engine starts to get too hot. You watch the temperature gauge go up and up, but you don't do anything about it. All of a sudden steam starts shooting out from under the hood, and the car quits! What should you do?

SPEEDING UP:

- How could you have kept the car from quitting?
- How is an overheated engine like an angry person?
- What situations in your family get you "overheated" with anger?

LOOK AT THE MAP:

Ephesians 4:26: "'In your anger do not sin': Do not let the sun go down while you are still angry."

TRAVEL PLAN:

Pretend you're going to invent a "temper gauge" each person in your family can wear to show how angry that person is at any moment. What would it look like? How would it work? How could you use it to make sure you don't let the sun go down on your anger?

See also "The Last Popsicle and Front Seats," page 54

What a Drive!

JUMP START:

Today you are beginning an adventure beyond your wildest dreams! Imagine that God has written a book about where you're going and what will happen to you, and it's on the best-seller list in heaven. (After all, He does have a wonderful plan for your life.) He is excited about seeing His book of your life unfold in real life! What's that book? What's the adventure?

SPEEDING UP:

- God's plan for you is an adventure. What might it contain?
- Imagine the best possible adventure for you; what would it be like?
- What could interfere with you having this adventure?

LOOK AT THE MAP:

Ephesians 1:11: "In [Christ] we were also chosen ... according to the plan of him who works out everything in conformity with the purpose of his will."

TRAVEL PLAN:

Adventurous travelers need a guide. Who would you choose? Why? How can you always try to follow God's plan? Sometimes great adventures turn out differently from how people expect them to. How can you stay on the right course?

See also "Wet Pavement Ahead," page 40

Drive-Thru Surprise

JUMP START:

It's not a dream. Mom said you guys needed a bite of lunch, so she stopped at Fast Food Joe's. Next thing you remember is pulling the tab off your root beer can, and guess what?! You won the grand prize of one million dollars! What are the first things you would want to spend your money on?

SPEEDING UP:

- What would be some wise ways to use your money?
- Who would you share your money with? Why?

LOOK AT THE MAP:

Second Corinthians 8:7: "Just as you excel in every-thing—in faith, in speech, in knowledge, in complete earnest-ness and in your love for us—see that you also excel in this grace of giving."

TRAVEL PLAN:

Say you have to keep on giving after you've blown your million. What would you give?

See also "Topical Bible Blitz—Money," page 74

GIVING

Identity Crisis

JUMP START:

Okay, you've gone to the mall to get some new school clothes. You all get a little hungry, so you decide to stand in line to buy some fries. Suddenly Ronald McDonald runs into the food court, leaps over the counter, grabs a burger, jumps back over the counter, and runs back outside! What would you think?

SPEEDING UP:

- Was that the real Ronald? Why or why not?
- Say you're accused of stealing. What would a character witness say in your defense?
- Who was affected by Ronald's theft?

LOOK AT THE MAP:

Exodus 20:15: "You shall not steal."

TRAVEL PLAN:

Say Ronald was convicted of stealing and betraying children everywhere. You have to help him become an honest man. What would you tell him to do? How could he right his wrong?

See also "Fire Trucks on the Move!" page 45

Going Back in Time

JUMP START:

Today your vehicle is a time machine. Imagine that you could drive back into the past and choose your identity. You could be absolutely anyone from the Bible. Who would you be? Why?

SPEEDING UP:

Think about your character.

- Have you ever wondered why that person made some of the choices he or she made? Put yourself in the person's shoes to see if you can figure it out.

- What is your favorite part of the story or stories that your character was involved in?

- What is one choice he or she made that you would have done differently? Why?

LOOK AT THE MAP:

Psalm 106:3: "Blessed are they who maintain justice, who constantly do what is right."

TRAVEL PLAN:

Was your character able to learn from any mistakes? As your time machine comes back to the present, how can you be like your Bible character in your own life?

See also "The Traveling Junk Man," page 42

Pray Your Way Home

JUMP START:

In *The Wizard of Oz*, Dorothy and her dog, Toto, are spun away in a tornado to a strange new land. She and her new friends follow the yellow brick road, searching desperately for the Wizard. Dorthy has been told that he can send her home. After going through many troubles, they find that the Wizard has no special powers at all! What would you have done if you had been Dorothy?

SPEEDING UP:

- How does talking to the Wizard compare to praying?
- How is God like or unlike the Wizard?
- What is one thing you would like from God that money can't buy? Courage? A "heart"? Self-control? Why?

LOOK AT THE MAP:

First Peter 5:7: "Cast all your anxiety [worries] on him because he cares for you."

TRAVEL PLAN:

Prayer is simply talking to God about what's on your heart. Retell the *Wizard of Oz* story—this time with Dorothy praying to God for help. How might the story turn out differently?

See also "Topical Bible Blitz—Prayer," page 78

Fit for the Ride?

JUMP START:

How well do you do biking, walking, or running? On a scale from 1 to 10, how physically fit are you? If you were 100 percent fit, what would you do differently?

SPEEDING UP:

Being physically fit is one of many areas in your life that requires self-discipline.

- What kind of shape do you imagine that Jesus was in? Why?
- What other things in life require self-discipline? (Hint: think trash, homework, sleep, kindness.)

LOOK AT THE MAP:

Hebrews 12:11: "No discipline seems pleasant at the time, but painful. Later on, however, it produces a harvest of righteousness and peace for those who have been trained by it."

TRAVEL PLAN:

Design fitness plans to turn a couch potato into an Olympic athlete, a neighborhood hero, a prayer warrior. What kinds of things would be in each plan? What would not?

See also "Another Run Driven In!" page 49

Run for Your Life

JUMP START:

You may be familiar with *The Tale of Peter Rabbit* in which Peter disobeyed his mother—big time! Naughty Peter was tempted by the goodies in the garden and narrowly escaped becoming Mr. McGregor's supper. He was really traveling to get out of harm's way! Just glad to be alive and back in his own home, he accepted his dose of medicine and went to bed early. If you had been Peter, would you have learned a lesson?

SPEEDING UP:

- How well do you follow directions? Name three situations that could end up deadly if there is not complete obedience.
- Peter's downfall was the garden. What's your "garden"?
- How do you get in trouble in it?

LOOK AT THE MAP:

Ephesians 6:1–3: "Children, obey your parents in the Lord, for this is right. 'Honor your father and mother'—which is the first commandment with a promise—'that it may go well with you and that you may enjoy long life on the earth.'"

TRAVEL PLAN:

Imagine your backyard is full of all the things that tempt you to disobey. They're coming to life and are out to get you. You have to get through the yard safely. What do you need to help you? (A shovel to bury stuff? Determination? A cell phone to call for help?) Ready? Run for your life!

See also "Another Run Driven In!" page 49

Wet Pavement Ahead

JUMP START:

Have you ever noticed a section of sidewalk or a driveway where something or someone accidentally squished the concrete before it dried? Wet concrete is a little like the wet clay that the Bible talks about. What condition does either clay or concrete need to be in to accomplish shaping it into anything worthwhile?

SPEEDING UP:

- What would have been the smart thing to do if the workers didn't want anyone messing up their smooth sidewalk before it dried?

- What similarities do people have with clay?

- Can you imagine God as a great potter? What are some ways that God molds people?

- God wants to mold our characters to be like His Son. What qualities does Jesus have that God wants us to have?

LOOK AT THE MAP:

Ephesians 2:10: "We are God's workmanship, created in Christ Jesus to do good works, which God prepared in advance for us to do."

TRAVEL PLAN:

What attitudes and actions can make you like moldable clay to God? Like hard pavement? Having God's tire tracks showing up in your pavement is a good thing.

See also "Off to the Video Arcade?" page 48

The Overflowing Lot

JUMP START:

Have you ever gone to a circus or the Ice Capades or some other huge show? Imagine how many people have to be involved in planning and actually pulling off big events. Just think, for instance, if the advertising person had forgotten to let people know what had been planned. What probably would have happened?

SPEEDING UP:

The body of Christ is made up of all His followers, and each one has a part to contribute.

- What's your part?
- How could you make Sunday morning at our church into a sellout? What kinds of help would you need? Who would you ask?
- What would our family members contribute?

LOOK AT THE MAP:

First Corinthians 12:27: "Now you are the body of Christ, and each one of you is a part of it."

TRAVEL PLAN:

Think about our family's part in the body of Christ. What difference does it make that our vehicle is in the church parking lot?

See also "Topical Bible Blitz—Body of Christ," page 79

The Traveling Junk Man

JUMP START:

Imagine you are the nationwide "media garbage expert." You travel the nation, instructing everyone to make two gigantic stacks of stuff. In one stack you want the good, humorous, fun, healthy, wholesome, and godly stuff (neatly arranged, of course). In the other stack they are to put everything else. Which stack is likely to be the bigger? Why?

SPEEDING UP:

- Brainstorm some "guru guides" that will help people decide which pile to put things in.
- If you can think of your mind like a sponge, what kind of "water" are you soaking up?

LOOK AT THE MAP:

Philippians 4:8: "Whatever is true, whatever is noble, whatever is right, whatever is pure, whatever is lovely, whatever is admirable—if anything is excellent or praiseworthy—think about such things."

TRAVEL PLAN:

Apply your "guru guides" to your room. What gets thrown out? What about using the "guru guides" on your mind? Your mouth? Someone has come up with some great "guru guides" already—God. How can you decide in your own life if it's time to throw something in the junk pile?

See also "Stumbling Is No Fun," page 51

DISCERNMENT

Driving in a Hurricane

JUMP START:

Ever driven through a hurricane? The lightning flashes, the rain pelts your car so hard you can't hear each other yell, and the wind rocks your car. The hair on your body stands on end from the electricity in the air—or is it fear? You're hanging on for dear life. A shiver runs up your spine as the power of the terrible storm batters your vehicle. It's fear, all right! What is the scariest situation you have ever been in?

SPEEDING UP:

- When you are scared, what do you do?
- There are lots of Bible stories where people were in scary situations. Name as many as you can think of.
- How did those people conquer their fear? Was there a hero who rescued them?

LOOK AT THE MAP:

Psalm 28:7: "The LORD is my strength and my shield; my heart trusts in him, and I am helped."

TRAVEL PLAN:

If you were given a storm warning for your life, what might the "storm" be? What difficult things are coming up? Plan ahead; how can you make it through the storms that might come?

See also "Moving at the Speed of Light," page 53

Mapping the Treasure

JUMP START:

Imagine that you had the job of giving your visiting cousins detailed directions to find the best ice cream in town, the best vacation spot ever, or some other "treasure" of your choice. How would you do it? What methods would you use?

SPEEDING UP:

God had an even bigger treasure to share with us. He wrote down His directions for us in the Bible.

- What treasure does the Bible give directions to? How do you find this treasure?

- How can you know the Bible is God's instruction book to the treasure?

LOOK AT THE MAP:

Psalm 119:89–90: "Your word, O LORD, is eternal; it stands firm in the heavens. Your faithfulness continues through all generations."

TRAVEL PLAN:

Describe to someone how to find the following: the spare tire, kindness, your school, your best friend's house, generosity, your garage, Jesus.

See also "About the Bible Trivia," page 59

Fire Trucks on the Move!

JUMP START:

Have you ever wondered where those fire trucks are headed in such a hurry? In the United States more than 2.4 million fires occur yearly, causing around six thousand deaths, thousands of injuries, and billions of dollars of damage. Many of these fires have been started on purpose. Talk about a bad attitude leading to trouble! What bad attitudes might cause people to commit crimes like this?

SPEEDING UP:

- Fire destroys things and is dangerous. What do you do if you're in a building where a fire starts? How do you put fires out?

- How are fires like sin? Imagine sin is like a fire in the "building" of your life. How can you avoid it or put out those "sin" fires?

- Fire prevention leads to safety. What good results come from doing "sin prevention" in your life?

LOOK AT THE MAP:

First John 1:9: "If we confess our sins, he is faithful and just and will forgive us our sins and purify us from all unrighteousness."

TRAVEL PLAN:

Pretend you're a sin fighter speaking to kids in schools about how to be safe from sin fires. What would you tell them?

See also "Topical Bible Blitz—Salvation," page 76

Sunroofs or Plush Seats?

JUMP START:

What would you absolutely insist on having if you were old enough and had money to buy a car? Would you want it to be a certain color or style? Would you buy something simple so that you could save your money for other priorities, or would you get something really fancy?

SPEEDING UP:

• What kind of car should Christians buy?

• Besides choosing different cars, Christians also dress differently and listen to different styles of music. How else are they different?

• How can we know if what someone believes is okay or not?

LOOK AT THE MAP:

First Corinthians 12:12: "The body is a unit, though it is made up of many parts; and though all its parts are many, they form one body. So it is with Christ."

TRAVEL PLAN:

Some car parts are optional (sunroofs may be great for some people, but they're not for everyone). Other parts aren't. Can you name certain parts that a car has to have if it's going to run? What things do people have to have or do if they say they're Christians?

See also "The Traveling Junk Man," page 42

DIFFERING BELIEFS

Can't Wait to Drive?

JUMP START:

At last the day has arrived! You have just passed your driver's license exam and you are handed the keys to your parents' brand-new ZXT 4000. What do you think it will be like when you are given the keys for the first time, and where would you want to go first?

SPEEDING UP:

- Why might your parents trust you with their car? What do you think their idea of the perfect driver is?

- Name some of your responsibilities that you feel you carry out well. Are there areas you don't feel so great about?

- How do you feel when you have done what was expected of you?

LOOK AT THE MAP:

Luke 16:10: "Whoever can be trusted with very little can also be trusted with much, and whoever is dishonest with very little will also be dishonest with much."

TRAVEL PLAN:

Your day to drive your family's car is coming—sooner than you imagine! What can you do in the next few years to convince your parents they could trust you with their car?

See also "Fit for the Ride?" page 38

Off to the Video Arcade?

JUMP START:

If you could design the most fantastic, fun, exciting video game that was ever made, what would it be like?

SPEEDING UP:

- What lessons have you learned or seen friends learn from playing video games?

- You probably listed "growing as a Christian" as one of the results of playing video games. What?! You didn't?! Why not?

- If you don't think that you grow in Christ by playing video games, then just how does a person grow in Christ?

LOOK AT THE MAP:

Psalm 25:5: "Guide me in your truth and teach me, for you are God my Savior, and my hope is in you all day long."

TRAVEL PLAN:

Have you measured your height to see if you're growing lately? How about measuring your growth in Christ? Think about it. How would you measure it? Video games or not, we want to be growing in Christ each day.

See also "Wet Pavement Ahead," page 40

Another Run Driven In!

JUMP START:

"The bases are loaded, the final batter is up." You've heard these phrases if you listen to ball games on the car radio or watched them on television. Many boys look at their major-league heroes and dream about being in the majors someday too. To be a really great ball player requires a lot of hard work and determination. What is it about your favorite ball players or musicians or movie stars that makes them heroes to you? In what ways would you like to be like them? Why?

SPEEDING UP:

- Who are your heroes? Are they Christians?
- How can you be a hero? Who can you be a hero to?
- What would make older people look up to you as a hero?

LOOK AT THE MAP:

First Timothy 4:12: "Don't let anyone look down on you because you are young, but set an example for the believers in speech, in life, in love, in faith and in purity."

TRAVEL PLAN:

If you were a great ball player or a famous singer, what would you want a fan to say about you?

See also "Fit for the Ride?" page 38

Traveling Through Space

JUMP START:

Imagine for a moment that you could shift the car into "fly" right now and soar above the clouds! Looking out your window, you begin to wonder what it would be like to step out onto those fluffy puffs of white. They look like gigantic cotton balls in the sky—very beautiful up close. What do you think a cloud feels like?

SPEEDING UP:

- The Bible teaches us that Jesus returned to heaven on a cloud. Obviously He can do things that we can't do. What would you have been thinking if you had seen Him go that day?

- Do you look forward to the time when Jesus returns to take His people back to heaven with Him? Why or why not?

LOOK AT THE MAP:

First Corinthians 15:51–52a: "Listen, I tell you a mystery: We will not all sleep, but we will all be changed—in a flash, in the twinkling of an eye, at the last trumpet."

TRAVEL PLAN:

To your knowledge, has anyone ever spotted heaven in a telescope? Why or why not?

For now we are given only a glimpse of heaven by reading the Bible, but we know one thing for sure—it'll be awesome! Describe heaven and what you think will be the best part. Traveling through space should be pretty cool too!

See also "Topical Bible Blitz—Heaven," page 75

Stumbling Is No Fun

JUMP START:

Have you ever been running so fast that you tripped and fell flat on your face? Ouch! Or been walking on a path that suddenly crumbled beneath your feet? Solomon wrote, "Make level paths for your feet and take only ways that are firm" (Proverbs 4:26). How can you avoid tripping or walking on crumbling roads again (besides taking a paving crew with you)? How is that like making solid "roads" in your everyday life?

SPEEDING UP:

Solomon requested wisdom, and God gave him lots of it! He wrote proverbs, or wise sayings, to help people think about wisdom and how to live wisely. Try figuring out these proverbs:

- "The path of the righteous is like the first gleam of dawn, shining ever brighter till the full light of day" (Proverbs 4:18).

- "As churning the milk produces butter, and as twisting the nose produces blood [Ouch!], so stirring up anger produces strife" (Proverbs 30:33).

- Wisdom doesn't always come easily—but it's worth it. Where could you use wisdom in your life? Where can you get it?

LOOK AT THE MAP:

Proverbs 2:6: "The LORD gives wisdom, and from his mouth come knowledge and understanding."

TRAVEL PLAN:

If you know you have the choice to drive on a paved road, a dusty gravel road, or a muddy swamp road, which would you take? Why? Your everyday choices take you down "roads" like these. How do you choose solid roads for your life?

See also "What a Drive!" page 33

Caught in a Speed Trap

JUMP START:

Occasionally people get pulled over by the police because they are driving too fast. Sometimes the driver of the vehicle totally disagrees with how fast the police say he was going. Describe a couple of different ways a conversation might go between a police officer and a driver—let's say it happens to be your dad this time. What might happen if your dad decides to yell and scream in protest?

SPEEDING UP:

- What difference would the way your dad speaks to the police make in how he is treated?
- Is a police officer someone who should be respected? Why or why not?
- What does respect look like? How do you recognize it when you see it?

LOOK AT THE MAP:

First Peter 2:17a: "Show proper respect to everyone."

TRAVEL PLAN:

Give ten reasons *you* should be respected. Name ten ways to be respectful. Now name ten people to whom you should show respect. How might a good attitude get you out of trouble?

See also "Run for Your Life," page 39

Moving at the Speed of Light

 JUMP START:

Imagine yourself having a secret identity with strength and powers beyond human abilities, such as the ability to soar through the air with lightning speed, X-ray vision to see through walls, strength to pick up buildings! What abilities would you want? What might you set off to do if you had those kinds of abilities?

SPEEDING UP:

- Know of anyone who has those kinds of abilities?
- Imagine a supervillain and a superhero. What do they do with their power?
- Power alone does not make you a superhero. You could be a supervillain. What makes the difference between a superhero and a supervillain?

LOOK AT THE MAP:

Psalm 147:5: "Great is our Lord and mighty in power; his understanding has no limit."

TRAVEL PLAN:

Okay, so God is the greatest superhero of all time! He's all-powerful and can do anything! So, what does He do with His power? He has X-ray vision, you know—what does He do with this ability? How does God's use of power help you trust Him?

See also "Driving in a Hurricane," page 43

The Last Popsicle® and Front Seats

JUMP START:

"I get the front seat!" "I was here first!" "It's mine!" "You had the last popsicle last time." "She's not sharing." "He hit me." Ah, the magical world of brotherhood and sisterhood. What would life be like if brothers and sisters always got along? Use your imagination.

SPEEDING UP:

- What are five nice things about having brothers or sisters? (Yes, there are nice things—lots of them.) Name them.

- Think of the last time you fought with your sibling. What was the result? How did you feel after? Who really won?

- When you argue or disagree, what is it that you *really* want? (Fairness? Respect?)

LOOK AT THE MAP:

Matthew 7:12: "Do to others what you would have them do to you."

TRAVEL PLAN:

Describe your ideal brother or sister. What would he or she do for you? How would he or she treat you? What's the best way to be treated nicely like that more often? How can *you* be the ideal brother or sister? Try it—backseats aren't so bad some of the time.

See also "Boiling Mad," page 32

Bible Challenges

Get Ready to Sharpen Your Bible Knowledge!

The first sections of Bible Challenges are organized with markings for difficulty:

E – Easy
M – Moderate
H – Hard

The answers are never far away. Simply flip back a page or two to the end of that section of trivia. You may wish to ask your younger children to answer the E questions, and older children to answer M or H questions, so that everyone has a fair chance at getting answers.

Competition scoring: If you have children who wish to compete for points, keep track of who gets the most answers correct and give one point to the winner at the end of each section of challenges.

Timed scoring: If the children aren't in the mood to compete, score one point to children in terms of how long they participate in the challenges. Give one point for each 10 minutes of participation.

Could Be Anything Bible Trivia

1. E – Who was Jesus' mother?
2. E – What is the Golden Rule?
3. E – Who betrayed Jesus?
4. M – During Jesus' final hours before He was arrested, He prayed earnestly. His sweat fell like what?
5. E – How many times did Peter deny Jesus?
6. H – What are precepts?
7. H – When the Amalekites came and attacked the Israelites, the key to Israel's success was for Moses to do this continually. What did he have to do?
8. M – What did Jesus say is the greatest commandment?
9. M – How many of the fruit of the Spirit can you name?
10. M – A cheerful heart is what, according to a proverb?

11. M – What color signifies royalty in the Bible?

12. E – What was the food that the Israelites ate each morning in the wilderness?

13. M – What did Jesus say is the second greatest commandment?

14. E – What was Paul's name before he became a Christian?

15. M – How many pieces of silver was Judas Iscariot given to betray Jesus?

16. H – What is the name given to a speech by Jesus recorded in Matthew 5–7?

17. M – The expression that people use, "doubting Thomas," comes from a reference to one of Jesus' disciples. Why?

18. H – In the Old Testament, if a servant loved his master so much that he wished to remain that master's slave for life, then the master would take that servant and do what?

19. M – What is the name of the mountain on which God gave Moses the Ten Commandments?

20. M – When did God send the Holy Spirit to indwell the early Christians?

21. H – What rots the bones, according to a proverb?

22. E – What group of people was the Old Testament about?

23. M – What does the name Peter mean?

24. M – After Jesus rose from the dead, He appeared to some of His disciples along a road to what town?

25. E – Who was the wisest man who ever lived?

26. H – According to the psalmist, what kind of tree will the righteous flourish like?

27. H – Who in the Bible used the expression "on the tip of my tongue"?

28. H – When the Israelites complained to Moses in the desert, God told Moses to speak to the rock and it would pour out water. Moses disobeyed God by doing what?

29. H – Who was told by God to go hide for awhile east of the Jordan and drink from the brook there? God took care of him by sending ravens twice a day, to bring him bread and meat to eat.

30. E – Who preached in the desert and ate locusts and wild honey?

31. M – After Adam and Eve had sinned in the garden, they were ashamed. What did they sew together to cover themselves?

32. M – What is the biblical word that involves going without food for a period of time on purpose?

33. H – Who prophesied to dry bones and they came to life by God's power?

34. M – When the Israelites left Egypt, what did God give them to follow in the daytime?

35. M – What guided the Israelites by night?

ANSWERS FOR COULD BE ANYTHING BIBLE TRIVIA

1. Mary (Matthew 1:18).
2. Do to others as you would have them do to you (Luke 6:31).
3. Judas Iscariot (Matthew 26:47–48).
4. Blood (Luke 22:44).
5. Three times (Matthew 26:75).
6. Laws, directions, or principles (Psalm 119:45–48).
7. Keep his hands held up. When he grew tired, Aaron and Hur held his hands up for him (Exodus 17:11–12).
8. To love the Lord your God with all your heart and with all your soul and with all your mind (Matthew 22:37).
9. Love, joy, peace, patience, kindness, goodness, faithfulness, gentleness, and self-control (Galatians 5:22).
10. Good medicine (Proverbs 17:22).
11. Purple (Judges 8:26).
12. Manna (Exodus 16:14–31).
13. To love your neighbor as yourself (Matthew 22:39).
14. Saul (Acts 13:9).
15. Thirty (Matthew 26:15).
16. The Sermon on the Mount (Matthew 5:1).
17. Thomas doubted (didn't believe) that Jesus had risen from

the dead until he saw Him with his own eyes and felt Jesus' scars with his own hands (John 20:24–27).

18. Pierce the servant's ear (Exodus 21:6).

19. Sinai (Exodus 19:20).

20. On the day of Pentecost (Acts 2:1).

21. Envy (Proverbs 14:30).

22. The Israelites (Exodus 19:1–6).

23. Jesus changed Simon's name to Peter, which means "rock" (Matthew 16:18).

24. Emmaus (Luke 24:13).

25. Solomon (1 Kings 3:12).

26. A palm tree (Psalm 92:12).

27. Job (Job 33:2).

28. He hit the rock twice with his staff. God still let the water pour out, but Moses never was allowed to enter the Promised Land because of his disobedience (Numbers 20:8–12).

29. Elijah (1 Kings 17:2–4).

30. John the Baptist (Matthew 3:4).

31. Fig leaves (Genesis 3:7).

32. Fasting (2 Samuel 12:16).

33. Ezekiel (Ezekiel 37:7).

34. A pillar of cloud (Exodus 13:21).

35. A pillar of fire (Exodus 13:21).

About the Bible Trivia

1. E – Which is larger, the Old Testament or the New Testament?

2. E – What are the first and the last books in the Bible?

3. M – What two books of the Bible are named after women?

4. M – How many books are there in the Old Testament?

5. E – What books of the Bible are called the Gospels?

6. M – What books are called the books of the Law or the Pentateuch?

7. H – The Bible was written down in the span of approximately how many years? A. 30; B. 500; C. More than 1,500.

8. M – What are epistles?

9. H – About how many people wrote the Bible? A. 100; B. 40–50; C. Fewer than 30.

10. H – What is the longest name in the Bible?

11. H – How many languages have parts of the Bible been translated into? A. 100–120; B. 1,000–1,200; C. Over 2,000.

12. M – How many books are in the New Testament?

13. H – What was the first English Bible called?

14. M – What material was the Bible probably first written on? A. Papyrus sheets; B. Gold plates; C. Newspaper.

15. M – Which of these writers do we know to be a Gentile? A. Matthew; B. Paul; C. Luke.

16. E – What book of the Bible tells of the beginning of mankind?

17. M – What book tells us the most about the early church?

18. M – What chapter is called the "love chapter"?

19. E – What book is the longest book of the Bible?

20. H – Which of these biblical towns have been excavated? A. Jericho; B. Nineveh; C. Babylon.

21. E – The writers of the Bible had various occupations. Which of the following was not an occupation of any writers? A. Doctor; B. Prophet; C. King; D. Shepherd; E. Fisherman; F. Data entry clerk; G. Tax collector.

ANSWERS FOR ABOUT THE BIBLE TRIVIA

1. The Old Testament is larger.

2. Genesis and Revelation.

3. Esther and Ruth.

4. Thirty-nine.

5. Matthew, Mark, Luke, and John.

6. Genesis, Exodus, Leviticus, Numbers, and Deuteronomy.

7. C. Most authorities agree—more than 1,500 years.

8. Letters.

9. B. Most authorities agree that at least 40 men wrote the Bible.

10. Maher-Shalal-Hash-Baz. Aren't you glad that's not your name? It is found in Isaiah 8:1.

11. C. Some authorities document parts of the Bible in over 2,100 languages. The whole Bible has been translated into almost 300.

12. Twenty-seven.

13. The Geneva Bible was written in English in 1560 and was the Bible that the Pilgrims first brought to America.

14. A. Papyrus sheets in a roll.

15. C. Luke.

16. Genesis.

17. Acts.

18. First Corinthians 13.

19. Psalms takes up the most pages of the Bible with 150 chapters. However, Jeremiah has more words! Go figure.

20. Trick question. A, B, and C are all correct. There are many other biblical towns that have been excavated as well.

21. F. Data entry clerk.

Time Line Testers

Read the following choices to another person. The correct answer is underlined.

WHO CAME FIRST?

- E – Adam or Eve?
- M – Jacob or Esau?
- E – Abraham or Adam?
- M – Paul or Isaiah?
- E – John the Baptist or Jesus?
- M – Daniel or Peter?

- M – <u>Noah</u> or Jonah?
- M – Matthew or <u>Jacob</u>?
- M – Isaac or <u>Ishmael</u>?
- M – <u>Samuel</u> or Solomon?

WHICH COMES FIRST IN THE BIBLE?

- M – The choosing of the 12 disciples or <u>Jesus' baptism</u>?
- E – The book of Revelation or the book of <u>Romans</u>?
- M – The book of <u>Ruth</u> or the book of Jeremiah?
- M – The book of <u>Leviticus</u> or the book of Joshua?
- H – Paul's conversion on the road to Damascus or the <u>Day of Pentecost</u>?
- E – The book of <u>1 Kings</u> or the book of Mark?
- M – The <u>feeding of the five thousand</u> or the Last Supper?
- H – The commandment "<u>You shall not murder</u>" or the commandment "You shall not steal"?
- H – The commandment "Honor your father and mother" or the commandment "<u>You shall have no other gods before me</u>"?
- M – The Tower of Babel or <u>the Flood</u>?
- M – A staff becoming a snake or <u>a snake causing someone to "stumble"</u> (Genesis 3)?
- H – God creating the fish of the sea or God creating <u>fruit-bearing plants</u>?
- M – The <u>12 plagues on Egypt</u> or the Israelites entering the Promised Land?
- E – <u>The Garden of Eden</u> or the Flood?
- M – Baby Moses floating in a basket or <u>Joseph being thrown into a pit</u>?
- M – <u>The crossing of the Red Sea</u> or Saul being anointed king?
- E – <u>Jesus' triumphal entry into Jerusalem</u> or the persecution of Christians?
- M – King Ahab or <u>King Solomon</u>?

- M – <u>Joshua leading the children of Israel into the Promised Land</u> or the anointing of King David?
- E – <u>Cain killing Abel</u> or John following Jesus?
- E – Elizabeth, Mary's cousin, giving birth to a baby or <u>the angel telling Mary that she was going to have a baby</u>?

Follow the Clue Trivia

In this section of Bible trivia, give children one clue at a time and allow them time to do some guessing at what the answer might be. Go on to the next clue only when they *really need it* to continue their guesses.

Four or five clues are given, from hard to easy. Younger children should be able to achieve most of the answers by the time you get to Clue 4.

WHO AM I?

Clue 1: I once ate honey from a lion's carcass.
Clue 2: I was set apart from birth as a Nazirite of God.
Clue 3: I lied about the source of my strength several times.
Clue 4: When my hair was cut, my strength left me.
   (Answer: Samson)

Clue 1: I fled from the first king of Israel when he tried to kill me.
Clue 2: My son Solomon built the temple of the Lord after my death.
Clue 3: I wrote many songs to God.
Clue 4: I once killed a giant with a small stone and slingshot.
   (Answer: King David)

Clue 1: I once was frantic when my child was missing.
Clue 2: My fiancé almost divorced me.
Clue 3: An angel spoke to me.
Clue 4: I had to give birth to my child in a stable.
   (Answer: Mary, the mother of Jesus)

Clue 1: Jesus scolded me for injuring someone with my sword.
Clue 2: I am a fisherman by trade.

Clue 3: Jesus gave me my new name.
Clue 4: I lied three times about knowing Jesus.
(Answer: Peter)

Clue 1: My sisters and I were good friends of Jesus.
Clue 2: My sister Mary loved to sit and listen to Jesus.
Clue 3: Jesus wept about me.
Clue 4: Jesus performed a great miracle before the crowd when He told me to come out of my grave!
(Answer: Lazarus)

Clue 1: I was blessed with many sons.
Clue 2: I deceived my own father when I tricked him into giving me the blessing that belonged to my brother.
Clue 3: One of my sons was sold by his brothers because they hated him.
Clue 4: My brother's name was Esau.
(Answer: Jacob)

Clue 1: I am very clever and crafty.
Clue 2: I cause people to stumble and fall.
Clue 3: I am no match for God's power.
Clue 4: I caused sin to enter the world when I tricked Eve.
(Answer: Satan)

Clue 1: I told Daniel the meanings of his dreams.
Clue 2: I told Zechariah that his wife, Elizabeth, would have a child, even though they were getting old.
Clue 3: I told Mary that she was going to have a son, sent from God, and she was to name him Jesus.
Clue 4: I am an angel.
(Answer: Gabriel)

Clue 1: I am from the land of Uz.
Clue 2: I thought these guys giving me advice were my friends, then I started to wonder.
Clue 3: When God finally came and spoke to me after all my cries, I worshiped Him and gave Him praise.
Clue 4: Almost everything I had was taken from me.
Clue 5: After my trial God gave me twice what I had before.
(Answer: Job)

Clue 1: My name means "paradise" or "bliss."
Clue 2: There is a river in me.
Clue 3: A serpent spoke with someone in me.
Clue 4: I was Adam and Eve's first home.
   (Answer: The Garden of Eden)

Clue 1: My name means "oil press," a device for squeezing the oil from olives.
Clue 2: I'm one of Jesus' favorite places.
Clue 3: Jesus brought His disciples here after the Last Supper to watch and pray.
Clue 4: Jesus was betrayed with a kiss here.
   (Answer: The Garden of Gethsemane)

Clue 1: I cannot be found on a map.
Clue 2: Gates must be entered to come here.
Clue 3: Only people who have trusted in God have seen me.
Clue 4: There is a Book of Life here that contains the name of every person who will ever live here.
Clue 5: God's people will live with Him forever here.
   (Answer: Heaven)

Clue 1: People traveled from all around to buy food here when there were many years without rain.
Clue 2: The children of Israel were slaves here.
Clue 3: Moses was raised here by Pharaoh's daughter.
Clue 4: God sent plagues to me to force Pharaoh to let His people go.
   (Answer: Egypt)

Clue 1: The temple of the Lord was built here.
Clue 2: Every year Mary and Joseph came here for the Feast of the Passover.
Clue 3: The triumphal entry of Jesus took place here.
Clue 4: Jesus was crucified outside my city walls.
   (Answer: Jerusalem)

Clue 1: My name means "house of food."
Clue 2: I am the home town of King David, and so I am called "the City of David."

Clue 3: Joseph and Mary came here to register and pay taxes.
Clue 4: Jesus was born here.
(Answer: Bethlehem)

Clue 1: Joshua met the commander of the "army of the Lord" near me.
Clue 2: Rahab and her household were spared destruction because she helped the Israelites here.
Clue 3: God told Joshua to march the people around my walls.
Clue 4: By faith, my walls fell.
(Answer: Jericho)

WHAT AM I?

Clue 1: I cannot speak or walk, but I do breathe.
Clue 2: I once had the heart of man within me.
Clue 3: I am familiar with the depths of the oceans.
Clue 4: I am among the largest of creatures.
Clue 5: I swallowed Jonah.
(Answer: The whale [or large fish])

Clue 1: Jesus sent two disciples to find me.
Clue 2: Balaam was rebuked by one of my family.
Clue 3: I am a gentle animal.
Clue 4: Jesus rode on my back.
(Answer: A donkey)

Clue 1: Gideon's men broke many jars when they used me.
Clue 2: I am used to alert people.
Clue 3: I am made of brass on an animal horn.
Clue 4: I am an instrument.
(Answer: A trumpet)

Clue 1: I would not exist if hands did not form me from a plant.
Clue 2: I was used in the Bible as a means of escape for both Saul and Moses.
Clue 3: Miriam watched me on the river.
Clue 4: Sometimes people like to put fruit in me or hang me from the ceiling with plants in me.
(Answer: A basket)

Clue 1: Judas threw me into the temple after he realized his sin of betraying Jesus.

Clue 2: The love of me is the root of all kinds of evil.

Clue 3: The Bible tells you not to be greedy for me.

Clue 4: The Old Testament tells you to give at least a tenth of me to God.

(Answer: Money)

Clue 1: I am needed for life.

Clue 2: I am an important ingredient in baptism services.

Clue 3: In the first of the nine plagues in Egypt, I was changed to blood.

Clue 4: John 4:14: "Whoever drinks the ____ I give will never be thirsty."

(Answer: Water)

Clue 1: I am found in the books of Exodus and Deuteronomy.

Clue 2: God gave me to someone on a mountain.

Clue 3: I was written on stone.

Clue 4: You are to obey me.

(Answer: The Ten Commandments)

Clue 1: I am more precious than rubies.

Clue 2: If you lack me, you should ask God for me.

Clue 3: Luke 2:52: "Jesus grew in ____ and stature, and in favor with God and men."

Clue 4: Solomon asked God for me, and God granted his request.

(Answer: Wisdom)

Bible Riddles

Question: What did the baby say to the mommy?

Answer: "We will not all sleep, but we will all be changed" (1 Corinthians 15:51).

Question: What two "seas" never had boats sailing in them?

Answer: The Saddu-cees and the Phari-sees.

Question: When God created the earth, what team sport were the angels playing?

Answer: Baseball. Genesis 1:1 says, "In the big-inning."

Question: What do you give a Philistine with big feet?
Answer: Plenty of room!

Question: What do you call an animal with a long trunk who's been stuck in the ark for many weeks?
Answer: An eager elephant!

Question: What are two things Adam didn't eat for breakfast?
Answer: Lunch and dinner.

Question: If you drop a white hat into the Red Sea, what does it become?
Answer: Wet.

Question: What's the difference between a fish and David's harp?
Answer: You can't tuna fish.

Question: What did Eve call shoes made from banana skins?
Answer: Slippers.

Question: Why was the elephant almost late for the ark?
Answer: He forgot his trunk.

Question: What happened when five hundred hares got loose in the center of Jerusalem?
Answer: The guards had to comb the area.

Question: What did the large fish eat after spitting out Jonah?
Answer: Fish and ships.

Question: What do Winnie-the-Pooh and John the Baptist have in common?
Answer: Their middle name.

Question: What part of a fish did Peter find weighs the most?
Answer: The scales.

Question: Who was the shortest man in the Bible?
Answer: Knee-high Miya (Nehemiah).

Question: Who played tennis in the Bible?
Answer: David; he served in King Saul's court.

Topical Bible Blitz

This section of questions deals a little more directly with specific topics. The topic, Scripture passages, relevant questions, and the answers are all included to comprise the topical Bible knowledge. Use these questions to get started in spiritual conversations with your children.

OBEDIENCE

Philippians 2:14–15: "Do everything without complaining or arguing, so that you may become blameless and pure, children of God."

1. True or false: Jesus said, "If you obey My commands, you will receive many riches."

2. True or false: Abraham obeyed God, even to the point of sacrificing his own son, if necessary.

3. True or false: Samuel thought his mother was calling him at night, until he realized it was really Eli.

4. Jesus told a parable about two sons who were each told to do something. The first son said he wouldn't do it, but then changed his mind and obeyed. What happened with the second son?

   A. He said that he would obey, but he didn't; B. He went to his mother and asked her to help him; C. He did exactly what he was told to do.

5. True or false: Jesus didn't always obey His Father.

6. True or false: Members of your family never have problems with disobedience. They *always* obey and get along!

ANSWERS FOR OBEDIENCE:

1. False (John 15:10).

2. True (Genesis 22:12).

3. False (1 Samuel 3:4–5).

4. A. The second son failed to obey as he had promised (Matthew 21:31).

5. False (John 8:28–29).

6. It is unlikely anyone would dare to say "true" to this one. Why?

TEMPTATION

First Corinthians 10:13b: "God is faithful; he will not let you be tempted beyond what you can bear. . . . He will also provide a way out so that you can stand up under it."

1. Satan told Jesus to prove that He was the Son of God by turning something into bread. What was it?

   A. Fig leaves; B. Stones; C. Fish.

2. Next, Satan told Jesus to throw Himself down from where?

   A. A high cliff; B. A tall sycamore tree; C. The highest point of the temple.

3. Finally Satan took Him to the top of a very high mountain. What did Satan tell Jesus this time?

   A. To calm the sea below; B. That Jesus would receive all the kingdoms of the world if He would bow and worship Satan; C. That he hated Him.

4. True or false: Jesus picked up stones and threw them at Satan for trying to tempt Him.

5. Who were the first people to disobey God?

ANSWERS FOR TEMPTATION:

1. B. Stones (Matthew 4:3).

2. C. The highest point of the temple (Matthew 4:5).

3. B. That Jesus would receive all the kingdoms of the world if He would bow and worship Satan (Matthew 4:8–9).

4. False. He quoted the Scriptures each time (Matthew 4:4, 7, 10).

5. Adam and Eve (Genesis 3:6).

ANGELS

Hebrews 1:14: "Are not all angels ministering spirits sent to serve those who will inherit salvation?"

1. True or false: Jacob wrestled with an angel (in the form of a man) through the night.

2. True or false: Lucifer is a favored angel of God who is in charge of the angels in heaven today.

3. Whose face in the New Testament looked like the face of an angel when he spoke of God?

   A. Paul; B. Peter; C. Stephen.

4. Have you ever experienced something that gave you the feeling that an angel was guarding you or helping you? Talk about it.

ANSWERS FOR ANGELS:

1. True (Genesis 32:22–30; Hosea 12:2–4).

2. False. Satan was once the angel Lucifer. However, Lucifer tried to be greater than God. God cast Lucifer and his followers out of heaven. (Isaiah 14:12–15 describes the event.)

3. C. Stephen (Acts 6:15). Stephen was later stoned to death for speaking boldly about Christ.

4. If you have had an experience like this, you are not alone (see Hebrews 13:2).

THE THREE PERSONS OF GOD

Luke 3:21–22: "Jesus was baptized too. And as he was praying, heaven was opened and the Holy Spirit descended on him.... And a voice came from heaven; 'You are my Son, whom I love; with you I am well pleased.'"

1. Jesus gave instructions to His disciples before He went up to heaven. What did He tell them to do in the name of the Father, the Son, and the Holy Spirit?

   A. Baptize; B. Rebuke; C. Travel.

2. There is a common name that Christians use to describe the three persons of God who are one. This common name is found nowhere in the Bible. What is it?

   A. The Triangle; B. The Trinity; C. The Entity.

3. The first thing the Bible tells us that the Spirit of God did

was to: A. Cause rains to cover the earth; B. Hover over the waters; C. Inspire man to write the Bible.

4. True or false: Sometimes Jesus referred to the Holy Spirit as the "Omega."

5. What is the Aramaic term Jesus used for "Father"?
   A. Elohim; B. Jehovah; C. Abba.

6. Are there any special names that your family members use with one another?

Answers for the Three Persons of God:

1. A. Baptize (Matthew 28:19).

2. B. The Trinity.

3. B. Hover over the waters (Genesis 1:2).

4. False. Just try to find that in the Bible! Jesus referred to the Holy Spirit as the "Counselor" (John 16:7).

5. C. Abba (Mark 14:36).

6. Only you know the answer to this one. Junior, Sugar, Sweetie, and Buddy are among common answers.

Miracles of Jesus

John 20:30–31: "Jesus did many other miraculous signs in the presence of his disciples, which are not recorded in this book. But these are written that you may believe that Jesus is the Christ, the Son of God, and that by believing you may have life in his name."

1. Which miracle is told about in each of the four Gospels?
   A. Jesus' healing of the lepers; B. Jesus' healing of the woman who touched His clothes; C. The feeding of the five thousand with two fishes and five loaves of bread.

2. What was the first miracle Jesus did?
   A. He parted the Red Sea; B. He turned water into wine; C. He gave a blind man sight.

3. What did Jesus have to say to Peter after Peter came to Him on the water?
   A. "You of little faith"; B. "You just need to concentrate

on your own ability"; C. "Can't you trust Me for a second?"

4. Have you ever seen something happen that couldn't be explained in any other way, except to say that God did it?

ANSWERS FOR MIRACLES OF JESUS:

1. C. The feeding of the five thousand with two fishes and five loaves of bread (Matthew 14; Mark 6; Luke 9; John 6).

2. B. He turned water into wine (John 2:11).

3. A. "You of little faith, why did you doubt?" (Matthew 14:31).

4. Miracles didn't happen just in Jesus' day, you know! Talk about some very "ordinary" happenings that we take for granted and explain how God had to have done them.

GOD'S PLAN

Ephesians 5:15–17: "Be very careful, then, how you live—not as unwise but as wise, making the most of every opportunity, because the days are evil. Therefore do not be foolish, but understand what the Lord's will is."

1. Who did God choose to be the one to set His people free from slavery?

   A. Moses; B. David; C. Joseph.

2. True or false: The Lord told Jeremiah, "Before I created you, I wondered why you would be so stubborn."

3. This woman was the great-grandmother of David.

   A. Rebecca; B. Ruth; C. Sarah.

4. Why was Mary chosen by God to be the mother of Jesus?

   A. She had requested such a privilege of God; B. Mary was well recognized in her town for her great knowledge of God; C. Mary had found favor with God.

5. True or false: Esther used her position as queen to help save the Jews.

6. True or false: God uses ordinary people to do extraordinary things.

ANSWERS FOR GOD'S PLAN:

1. A. Moses (Exodus 3:10–11).

2. False. In reality, God told Jeremiah, "Before I formed you in the womb I knew you, before you were born I set you apart; I appointed you as a prophet to the nations" (Jeremiah 1:5).

3. B. Ruth (Ruth 4:13–22). Of course, it was in the family line of David that Jesus was eventually born. So, Ruth was the many-times-over great-grandmother of Jesus (about 30 generations, according to Matthew 1:17)!

4. C. Mary had found favor with God (Luke 1:30).

5. True (Esther 8:3–8).

6. True. Talk about how God used you or your family in a special way recently.

MONEY

Exodus 23:19: "Bring the best of the firstfruits of your soil to the house of the LORD your God." Romans 13:7: "Give everyone what you owe him."

1. Where did Jesus tell Peter to find a four-drachma coin to pay the taxes?

   A. In a fish; B. Under a stone; C. From the beggar at the temple.

2. What type of debt should we try to be in?

   A. Owing the bank lots of money; B. Owing love to others; C. Always borrowing more than we can repay.

3. What was the name of the celebration each year when the Israelites were to bring the firstfruits of their crops to the Lord?

   A. The Feast of Harvest; B. The Feast of Sacrifice; C. The Passover.

4. True or false: Everything belongs to God, ultimately, except for your possessions.

5. When we give, we are to be: A. Humorous; B. Stingy; C. Cheerful.

6. The last time you gave money or help to someone who needed it, how did you feel?

ANSWERS FOR MONEY:

1. In a fish's mouth (Matthew 17:27).
2. B. Owing love continually (Romans 13:8).
3. A. The Feast of Harvest (Exodus 23:16).
4. False (Psalm 24:1).
5. C. Be a cheerful giver (2 Corinthians 9:7).
6. Hope it made you feel happy, because if so, it makes God happy (2 Corinthians 9:7)!

HEAVEN

Philippians 3:20: "Our citizenship is in heaven. And we eagerly await a Savior from there, the Lord Jesus Christ."

1. The book of Revelation uses lots of symbols to describe the end times and heaven. Revelation uses a particular number a lot. What is it?

    A. 7; B. 14; C. 21.

2. Elijah and Enoch have something in common. What is it?

    A. They both didn't wear shoes; B. They both prophesied about heaven; C. They both didn't experience death.

3. True or false: Jesus has a place in heaven at God's left hand.

4. Which of the following won't be found in heaven?

    A. Tears; B. Death; C. Mourning, D. Pain; E. All of these.

5. Is there anyone in heaven right now whom you look forward to seeing someday?

ANSWERS FOR HEAVEN:

1. A. 7 (Revelation 1:4, 16, 20; 4:5; 5:6; 6:1; etc.).
2. C. They never experienced death, but were simply "taken" away to heaven (Genesis 5:24; 2 Kings 2:11).
3. False. Jesus' place is at God's *right* hand (Mark 16:19).
4. E. All of these won't be found in heaven (Revelation 21:4).

5. Jesus is there right now, waiting to see *you*!

SALVATION

Romans 1:16: "I am not ashamed of the gospel, because it is the power of God for the salvation of everyone who believes: first for the Jew, then for the Gentile."

1. True or false: The few people who have never sinned will be given special recognition in heaven.

2. The moment that Jesus died for our sins, something strange happened. What was it?

   A. The sun became bright; B. The rooster crowed; C. The curtain of the temple tore.

3. We are told in the Bible to wear the whole armor of God. What piece of the armor is salvation?

   A. Helmet; B. Sword; C. Breastplate.

4. What spiritual "drink" are new believers to crave like some people crave a chocolate bar?

   A. Wine; B. Milk; C. Grape juice.

5. A mother doesn't give a little baby a cheeseburger until the baby's old enough to eat it. In the same way, a teen-ager doesn't go around drinking warm milk from a bottle for his dinner. What does this idea have to do with new believers?

ANSWERS FOR SALVATION:

1. False. All have sinned (Romans 3:23), except Jesus.

2. C. The temple curtain tore (Matthew 27:51).

3. A. Helmet (Ephesians 6:17; 1 Thessalonians 5:8).

4. B. Pure spiritual milk (1 Peter 2:2).

5. In Hebrews 5:14 we read that as we grow in our spiritual life we mature from milk to solid food.

PARABLES OF JESUS

Luke 8:10a: "[Jesus] said, 'The knowledge of the secrets of the kingdom of God has been given to you.'"

1. True or false: Parables are easily understood by anyone.
2. Which parable involved a fattened calf?

   A. The parable of the shrewd manager; B. The parable of the good Samaritan; C. The parable of the lost (prodigal) son.
3. Jesus told a parable of a farmer who went out to sow his seed in different kinds of soil, which resulted in differing outcomes. This parable is often called "The Parable of the Sower." What does the seed represent in this parable?

   A. The Word of God; B. The man's wages; C. Good deeds.
4. Jesus told a parable about a hidden treasure. Where was the treasure hidden?

   A. At the bottom of the sea; B. In a man's closet; C. In a field.
5. Jesus said the kingdom of heaven is like a merchant looking for what?

   A. Fine pearls; B. A place to lay his head; C. Silver and gold.
6. True or false: The parable of the good Samaritan is named that way because the Samaritan was kind to a little girl who had no home.
7. What experiences have you had in which you had opportunity to be a "good Samaritan"?

ANSWERS FOR PARABLES OF JESUS:
1. False. In Luke 8:10b, Jesus states the sad truth that those who are not willing to receive Jesus' message will not be able to understand the meaning of the parables.
2. C. The prodigal son (Luke 15:23).
3. A. The Word of God (Luke 8:11).
4. C. In a field (Matthew 13:44).
5. A. Fine pearls (Matthew 13:45).
6. False (Luke 10:33).
7. After talking about them, see if you find an opportunity today to be a "good Samaritan."

SERVICE

Ephesians 4:12: "To prepare God's people for works of service, so that the body of Christ may be built up."

1. What act of service did Jesus do for His disciples before they ate their last Passover meal together?

    A. Cleared the dishes; B. Washed their feet; C. Poured expensive perfume on their heads.

2. What did Jesus tell His disciples they must do to become great?

    A. Give all their money to the poor; B. Be servants to others; C. Never gossip.

3. True or false: Many who are first will be last, and the last will be first.

4. In what way has someone who is in the car with you right now done a service for you lately?

ANSWERS FOR SERVICE:

1. B. He washed their feet (John 13:4–5).

2. B. They must be servants to others (Mark 10:43).

3. True (Mark 10:31).

4. After you have a chance to explain what a help it was to you, you'll have a chance to thank them.

PRAYER

Philippians 4:6b: "In everything, by prayer and petition, with thanksgiving, present your requests to God."

1. In the Old Testament, the Israelites were to direct their prayers toward this place.

    A. The temple in Jerusalem; B. Up toward heaven; C. Their pastureland.

2. True or false: The Bible tells us to pray until we grow weary.

3. What must you do so that "the door will be opened to you"?

    A. Shout; B. Knock; C. Ring the bell.

4. Have you experienced God answering prayer in your life?

1. A. The temple in Jerusalem (1 Kings 8:29).
2. False. Pray continually (1 Thessalonians 5:17)!
3. B. Knock (Luke 11:9).
4. Perhaps you *are* an answer to prayer! Talk about it.

BODY OF CHRIST

First John 1:7: "If we walk in the light, as he is in the light, we have fellowship with one another, and the blood of Jesus, his Son, purifies us from all sin."

1. True or false: Christians should not criticize each other.
2. When the Israelites were in the wilderness, God commanded that they worship in a special place. What was it?

   A. A boat at the mouth of the river; B. A cave in a mountain; C. The Tent of Meeting.
3. What should you not give up doing as some people do?

   A. Using good manners; B. Meeting together;
   C. Prophesying.
4. True or false: We should spur one another (ouch!) toward success and good deeds.
5. What does bad company corrupt?

   A. A good mind; B. Good intentions; C. Good character.
6. Which of your friends are good company for you to keep? Why?

ANSWERS FOR BODY OF CHRIST:

1. True (Romans 14:1–13).
2. C. The Tent of Meeting (Exodus 40:34–35).
3. B. Meeting together (Hebrews 10:25).
4. False. We should spur one another on toward love and good deeds (Hebrews 10:24).
5. C. Good character (1 Corinthians 15:33).
6. (Younger children should be encouraged to be as specific as possible about the friends' qualities.) Are any of them bad company?

Psalm 119:11: "I have hidden your word in my heart that I might not sin against you."

1. The Word of God is sharper than what?

   A. A double-edged sword; B. A razor; C. A Philistine spear.

2. John 3:16 is well known for what?

   A. Explaining the mysteries of the end times; B. Explaining the Gospel clearly; C. John baptizing Jesus.

3. Second Timothy 3:16 tells us four things that Scripture is useful for. They begin with the letters *t, r, c,* and *t.* Can you name these four things?

4. See if you can recite a Bible verse right now with its reference.

ANSWERS FOR BIBLE MEMORIZATION:

1. A. A double-edged sword (Hebrews 4:12).

2. B. Explaining the Gospel clearly.

3. Television, radio, CDs, and tapes—*not*. Teaching, rebuking, correcting, and training in righteousness.

4. Keep on hiding the Word in your heart!

PEACE

John 14:27: "Peace I leave with you; my peace I give you. I do not give to you as the world gives. Do not let your hearts be troubled and do not be afraid."

1. Who was the king of Salem who blessed Abraham and whose name means "king of peace"?

   A. Jeroboam; B. Melchizedek; C. Joash.

2. A woman once wet Jesus' feet with her tears and poured perfume on them. Jesus told her, "Your faith has saved you; go in peace." How did this woman get Jesus' feet dry?

   A. She blew gently on them; B. She used the hem of her skirt; C. She used her hair.

3. True or false: Hebrews 12:14a says, "Make every effort to live in quietness with all men and to be jolly."

4. Can you talk about what peace is?

PERSECUTION

Matthew 5:10: "Blessed are those who are persecuted because of righteousness, for theirs is the kingdom of heaven."

1. What good things are produced by going through hard times?

   A. Character and hope; B. Character and conscience; C. Distinction and hope.

2. What are you to do about people who persecute you (treat you really bad) because of Christ?

   A. Laugh at them and then pray for them; B. Tell them God loves them and then give them a bloody nose; C. Pray for them and bless them.

3. What was Jesus' prayer on the cross for the people who persecuted Him?

   A. Forgive them; B. Make them pay for this; C. Teach them a lesson.

4. Jesus says you are _____ when you are insulted and persecuted because of Him.

   A. Patient; B. Pitied; C. Blessed.

5. True or false: If you are persecuted because of Christ, you can look forward to a great reward in heaven.

6. Persecution is probably the *least* fun topic in this book. Why talk about it then?

2. C. Pray for them (Matthew 5:44) and bless them (Romans 12:14). How? Ask God for lots of help at a time like that!

3. A. "Father, forgive them, for they do not know what they are doing" (Luke 23:34).

4. C. Blessed (Matthew 5:11). Perhaps you are being patient and pitied as well?

5. True (Matthew 5:12).

6. You need to understand that you are never alone. Christ can be your strength and help in all times.

Bible Mysteries

The following stories are written like mysteries. Read them to your children and see if they can guess "Who done it?" or "What is it?" in the Bible. Pause briefly between the sentences to build the suspense. Older children might be able to guess the answer before you get to the end, while younger ones will want the chance to guess after the whole story has been read.

WHO DONE IT?

1. Now *there* was somebody that stood out in a crowd! We were camping on the hillside, just waiting till we were told what to do next. Then I heard all the commotion and saw this blinding light reflecting off this guy's body and head. He was covered in metal for protection. He was yelling and challenging anyone to a fight. *Are you kidding?* I thought to myself. Nobody knew what to do next. King Saul was really baffled. He wanted an end to the madness. Then an unexpected answer came in the form of a little boy. Who was the guy covered in metal who was causing the commotion?
   (Answer: Goliath)

2. We were just minding our own business that day—trying to earn a living. We had actually been up through the night working hard with nothing to show for it. We were putting all our gear away and cleaning up when this man came up and started talking to us. He was no ordinary

man. He told our partner, Simon, to try throwing the net out one more time. That's when Simon called for our help. His boat was practically sinking, there were so many fish caught in the net! Our father, Zebedee, was there with us. He probably would have thought we were up to no good if he hadn't seen the whole thing himself. Jesus later gave us the nickname "Sons of Thunder." I guess He thought that we knew how to cause a commotion! Can you guess who we are?

(Answer: We are brothers, James and John. Jesus called us to be two of His disciples.)

3. My wife and I were trying to raise our child as best we could. However, there were people who wanted to find us to harm our family. I obeyed when an angel came to me in a dream and told me to leave the country. We traveled in the night so we wouldn't be seen. We lived in peace for a while in a foreign land until the angel warned us that we needed to move on again. This happened several times, since danger followed us. We finally moved and settled in the town of Nazareth. We stayed here in safety as our family grew, and I worked hard as a carpenter to provide for them. Who am I?

(Answer: I am Joseph, Jesus' earthly "father.")

4. Everything happened so quickly, it seems. Things got so bad in our town. The famine was terrible! My husband and I took our sons to live in Moab, where we thought things would be better. However, my husband, whom I loved so much, died. I was left with my two sons. They both got married in that country. But then something terrible happened—both of my sons died too. I was overcome with sadness. I just wanted to go back to my homeland, where at least I felt like I belonged. One of my daughters-in-law came back with me. Do you know who I am?

(Answer: Naomi)

5. What an evil plot I was the object of! Because I was a Jew and refused to honor Haman, by bowing to him, I was sentenced to die. Haman was an evil man who was really out to kill the king. It was only by God's grace and the bravery of my cousin, Queen Esther, that my

people and I did not die. When the king finally realized that I was responsible for saving his own life, I was placed in a position of great honor and Haman was killed. Who am I?

(Answer: Mordecai)

6. There it stood, an amazing image 90 feet high, right in the middle of the plains. There were people milling around everywhere. Musicians stood to the side waiting for the cue to begin playing their instruments. We thought, *Wow, this is going to be some concert!* Then someone got up to speak. They said that when the music started to play, everyone must fall down on their knees and worship this . . . this thing! We looked at each other. All of us had our mouths wide open in disbelief! We said to each other, "He's got to be joking! We aren't bowing to anyone or anything but our Lord God!" Well, that's when the trouble began for us. We experienced some real heat, to be sure! But God is faithful to those who put their trust in Him. Who are we?

    (Answer: Shadrach, Meshach, and Abednego are the faithful friends of God who were thrown into a fiery furnace for refusing to bow to the golden image.)

7. We all set off together on a beautiful day for sailing. The ship was stocked with everything we needed. The passengers aboard paid decent money to take this ride across the Great Sea. Some of the passengers stayed up on the deck to see what was going on. A few went below to find a resting place. It wasn't long into the journey that a big wind began. The waves got big. The thunder rolled in and the sky grew dark. It was pretty scary as the ship was tossed about and water rolled onto the deck. We started throwing our supplies over the side of the ship to make it lighter. Maybe our anchor would hold if we could just lighten the ship enough. Then this guy who had been sleeping through all the commotion raised his hand and nodded, as if accepting the blame. We finally threw him overboard and everything calmed down. Who was this man?

    (Answer: Jonah.)

8. Azariah had been out of the city for seven years. As he walked across the yard he noticed that something had changed. Where there used to be nothing but broken ground, a building 90 feet long, 30 feet wide, and 30 feet tall stood. It was covered in gold inside and two huge bronze pillars guarded the entrance. *Who could have done this?* he wondered. *What is it?*

    (Answer: Solomon did it. He built God's temple in just over seven years.)

WHAT IS IT?

1. It was a miracle, you know. Incredible! Jesus was traveling, and He came to the place where ten men were shouting to Him. They must have heard stories about Jesus; otherwise, how would they have known to ask Him? Anyhow, they each had a terrible skin disease. So they wanted Jesus to have pity on them and heal them. Jesus told them to go and show themselves to the priests. As soon as they turned and headed away, they were healed. They were so happy. I just don't understand why they all didn't come back to thank Jesus. Only one of the men came back, thanked Jesus, and gave praise to God. Do you know what disease Jesus cured them of?

    (Answer: Leprosy)

2. My family and I couldn't believe our eyes. We had never seen anything like it before. You would think we would have been too preoccupied with clearing out our home that we had lived in for the past months to notice, but we had to take note. Formed by the combination of moisture and sunlight, this was something that really couldn't be measured. God told us this would be a sign for future generations. Some people sign a contract with their signature; other contracts may have a seal. This is a most unusual "signature." What is it?

    (Answer: A rainbow)

3. I am spoken of so often,
    And thought of oh, so highly.
    I am life and I am from the rock
    And I will be in heaven.

On earth I am desired far above the gold.
People draw me and they throw me out
When they need of me no more.
I once became the juice of grapes,
And once became as blood.
Can you guess just who I am
From all the clues above?
(Answer: Water)

4. This is a riddle you must guess,
It is not sweet, now you can test.
Our God has called us this to be
We in the world so others see.
It cannot grow, it cannot breathe;
A pillar once it did achieve.
You may not have it in your car,
Just stop for food and don't look far.
What is it?
(Answer: Salt)

Interest Index

When your child is interested in a certain topic or is dealing with a specific issue, look it up here and you will be directed to relevant games (G), discussion starters (D), and/or challenges (C).

"On the Way to..." Index

When you're ready to jump in the car and want to talk about something related to where you are headed, check here for the place you're off to and then go to the item listed.

WEDDING
God's Plan for You D 33
Here's a Pair, There's a Pair
G 24

Topical Index

Welcome to the Family!

Heritage Builders

Helping You Build a Family of Faith

We hope you've enjoyed this book. Heritage Builders was founded in 1995 by three fathers with a passion for the next generation. As a new ministry of Focus on the Family, Heritage Builders strives to equip, train and motivate parents to become intentional about building a strong spiritual heritage.

It's quite a challenge for busy parents to find ways to build a spiritual foundation for their families—especially in a way they enjoy and understand. Through activities and participation, children can learn biblical truth in a way they can understand, enjoy—and *remember.*

Passing along a heritage of Christian faith to your family is a parent's highest calling. Heritage Builders' goal is to encourage and empower you in this great mission with practical resources and inspiring ideas that really work— and help your children develop a lasting love for God.

***

How To Reach Us

For more information, visit our Heritage Builders Web site! Log on to **www.heritagebuilders.com** to discover new resources, sample activities and ideas to help you pass on a spiritual heritage. To request any of these resources, simply call Focus on the Family at 1-800-A-FAMILY (1-800-232-6459) or in Canada, call 1-800-661-9800. Or send your request to Focus on the Family, Colorado Springs, CO 80995. In Canada, write Focus on the Family, P.O. Box 9800, Stn. Terminal, Vancouver, B.C. V6B 4G3

To learn more about Focus on the Family or to find out if there is an associate office in your country, please visit www. family.org

We'd love to hear from you!

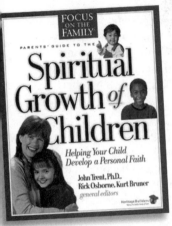

The Singing Bible

Children ages 2 to 7 will love *The Singing Bible,* which sets the Bible to music with over 50 fun, sing-along songs! Lead your child through Scripture by using *The Singing Bible* to introduce Jonah and the Whale, the Ten Commandments and more. This is a fun, fast-paced journey kids will remember!

Your Heritage

Ensure that the heritage you pass along to your children is a positive one. *Your Heritage* will equip you to become intentional in creating a meaningful, spiritually rich, living and memory-building legacy that will make your kids *and* future generations proud. Paperback.

• • •

Visit our Heritage Builders Web site! Log on to **www.heritagebuilders.com** to discover new resources, sample activities, and ideas to help you pass on a spiritual heritage. To request any of these resources, simply call Focus on the Family at 1-800-A-FAMILY (1-800-232-6459) or in Canada, call 1-800-661-9800. Or send your request to Focus on the Family, Colorado Springs, CO 80995. In Canada, write Focus on the Family, P.O. Box 9800, Stn. Terminal, Vancouver, B.C. V6B 4G3.

Heritage Builders™

Helping You Build a Family of Faith

Every family has a heritage—a spiritual, emotional, and social legacy passed from one generation to the next. There are four main areas we at Heritage Builders recommend parents consider as they plan to pass their faith to their children:

Family Fragrance

Every family's home has a fragrance. Heritage Builders encourages parents to create a home environment that fosters a sweet, Christ-centered AROMA of love through Affection, Respect, Order, Merriment, and Affirmation.

Family Traditions

Whether you pass down stories, beliefs and/or customs, traditions can help you establish a special identity for your family. Heritage Builders encourages parents to set special "milestones" for their children to help guide them and move them through their spiritual development.

Family Compass

Parents have the unique task of setting standards for normal, healthy living through their attitudes, actions and beliefs. Heritage Builders encourages parents to give their children the moral navigation tools they need to succeed on the roads of life.

Family Moments

Creating special, teachable moments with their children is one of a parent's most precious and sometimes, most difficult responsibilities. Heritage Builders encourages parents to capture little moments throughout the day to teach and impress values, beliefs, and biblical principles onto their children.

We look forward to standing alongside you as you seek to impart the Lord's care and wisdom onto the next generation—onto your children.

Helping You Build a Family of Faith

L I G H T *wave*

building Christian faith in families

Lightwave Publishing is one of North America's leading developers of quality resources that encourage, assist, and equip parents to build Christian faith in their families. Their products help parents answer their children's questions about the Christian faith, teach them how to make church, Sunday school, and Bible reading more meaningful for their children, provide them with pointers on teaching their children to pray, and much, much more.

Lightwave, together with its various publishing and ministry partners, such as Focus on the Family, has been successfully producing innovative books, music, and games for the past 15 years. Some of their more recent products include the *Parents' Guide to the Spiritual Growth of Children*, *Mealtime Moments*, and *My Time With God*.

Lightwave also has a fun kids' web site and an Internet-based newsletter called *Tips and Tools for Spiritual Parenting*. For more information and a complete list of Lightwave products, please visit: **www.lightwavepublishing.com**.